Cont

Introduction	1
Rub-a-Dub-Dub	6
The Wheels on the Bus	7
Miss Mary Mack	8
Happy Birthday	9
Doggie Doggie	10
Mary Had a Little Lamb	11
Oh We Can Play on the Big Bass Drum	12
Twinkle, Twinkle Little Star	13
A Hunting We Will Go	14
Kookaburra	15
Ode to Joy	16
Do You Know the Muffin Man?	17
Old Bald Eagle	18
La Cucaracha	19
A Sailor Went to Sea	20
Are You Sleeping?	21
The Mulberry Bush	23
Old McDonald	24
Bim Bum Biddy	25
London Bridge	26
Jingle Bells	27
Tinga Layo	28
Itsy Bitsy Spider	29
We Wish You a Merry Christmas	30
Brahms Lullaby	31
Ninety-Nine Bottles	32
Jolly Old Saint Nicholas	33
Oh Susannah	34
Row Row Your Boat	35
Acka Backa	36
Hot Cross Buns	37
Bell Horses	38

The steel tongue drum (aka tong drum, tank drum, gluck-o-phone, hapi drum) and the handpan (aka hank drum, UFO drum, zen drum) are percussion musical instruments designed to help you focus on your feelings, sensations and body. You don't need classical music training or knowledge of music theory to play them. The main purpose is relaxation, meditation and traveling through your inner world.

No previous training or skills are necessary to enjoy these fascinating instruments. It is impossible to play them incorrectly. Anyone can play them: those who want to develop a good sense of rhythm and an ear for music, those who are seeking relaxation after a hard day at work, those who have always had an interest in learning how to play a musical instrument, and those who want to introduce something unusual into their lives and explore their inner selves.

Both instruments have a unique deep and long sound, and both will sound equally good whether under the experienced musician's hands or a beginner's. Playing the handpan/tongue drum is an intuitive experience which transcends gender, age, culture, and language. It is used by hobbyists, performers, music therapists, cancer patients, educators, and students. You can play it too!

The Handpan

The handpan was designed in Berne, Switzerland by Felix Rohner and Sabina Schärer of PANArt in 2000. The original handpan is famous for its beautiful and deep sound, and although the original instrument is no longer produced, demand for it continues to grow. For this reason, the original PANArt handpan is a collector's item, and often difficult to find.

The handpan is a steel instrument which is played while resting on the musician's lap. It is constructed from two joined and shaped solid steel sheets, sealed around the edges to create a hollow cavity inside, and hammered to create perfect tonal fields. It can produce seven to nine specific tones, but unlike the steel drums that are synonymous with Carribean music, the handpan goes through a special process called gas-nitriding which hardens the bowls to create an even more exquisite ethereal sound.

The creation of the handpan was based on the design of other instruments such as gongs, gamelan, ghatam, drums, and bells. The width of the instrument metal is approximately 1mm The drum vibrates and produces sound depending on the size and shape that is hammered into the steel. Accordingly, the tuning is a very technical and time consuming process. Normally, there are 9 notes: an eight note scale around the sides and a lower note in the middle. At the bottom of the instrument (known as the "Gu" side), a hole allows the sound to resonate and to be properly amplified thanks to the phenomenon known as Helmholtz Resonance in physics. This resonance that gives the handpan its distinctive sound is the same property that one experiences when blowing across the top of a glass bottle.

The Steel Tongue Drum

The steel tongue drum evolved from the handpan and the wooden tongue drum, which was invented by the Aztecs in Mexico. Other names used for this instrument are the log drum or tone drum. Traditionally the instrument was made from a hollowed log with tuned tongues. The modern version has tongues cut into the top and can be played with mallets, as well as one's hands. The steel tongue drum is a new invention and it is also called the tank drum because some drums were made from a gas tank.

The steel tongue drum gets its unique tone from the vibrations of its tongues of steel. Like the wooden version of this instrument, when the tongue is struck with the finger or a mallet, it vibrates, creating sound waves. The tongues are optimally shaped to achieve the perfect tone and are arranged in such a way that the surrounding notes are musically compatible with each other. By doing this, harmony is created between the notes generated from a particular tongue and the supporting notes of those surrounding it. The multiple harmonic overtones are similar to that of singing bowls or musical bells, and the drum's body creates a resonating chamber that adds depth to the sound.

Main Differences between the Steel Tongue Drum and the Handpan

Both the handpan and the steel tongue drum can be played with your hands and used in your lap. While each instrument has its own unique and special sound, there are some differences:

- The steel tongue drum's notes are sustained for longer periods, usually around 8 seconds. The handpan rings for approximately 4 seconds.
The handpan has hammered and distorted strike zones. The tongue drum has cut ones.

- A handpan is single-scale tuned and can never be re-tuned. However, while this is true of tongue drums, some new models have multi-scaled tongues that can be re-tuned by adjusting the magnet on the drum.
- The handpan is large (about 24 inches in diameter). The tongue drum is significantly smaller.
- Handpans are more expensive than tongue drums.
- A handpan is very fragile due to its light composite material and the hammered strikes zones. Tongue drums are made of steel.
- The handpan is of African origin, while the tongue drum originated in the Aztec civilization of Mexico.
- The handpan is played by hand, while the steel tongue-drum is sometimes played with mallets, producing a softer sound, almost like raindrops. However, experienced steel tongue drum players can play it using their hands or fingers.

Playing the Steel Tongue Drum

It is important to become acquainted with your steel tongue drum. The sound of the steel tongue drum comes from the vibration of the tongues or slits that are cut out of the top of the instrument.

Tongue drums differ from the handpan in the number of notes and the types of notes which are included on the instrument. Usually, it is a diatonic instrument with one octave plus several notes from other octaves or some chromatic notes. Some may have three C notes and not a single F note. Others have several chromatic notes included.

So while it is based on the regular major diatonic scale, it does not have the typical CDEFGAB arrangement: it can have missing notes, a few additional bass and treble notes placed further away from the main group, or the notes arranged in a variety of ways.

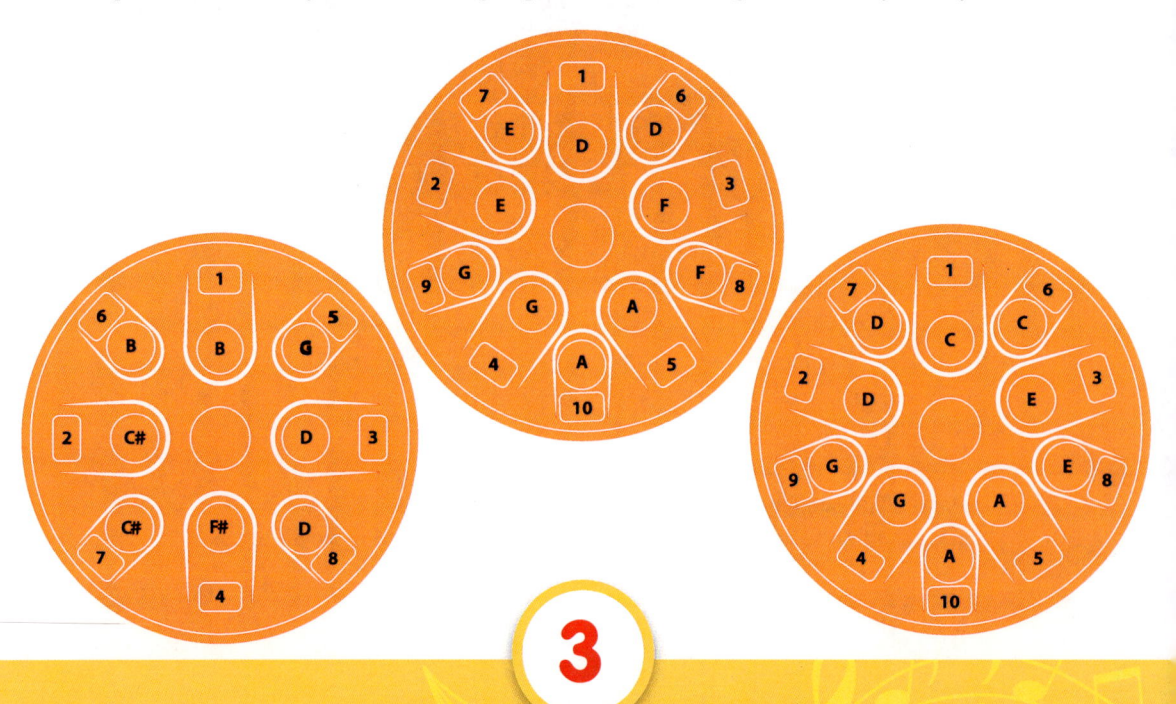

Most steel tongue drums come with mallets. In fact, if
you've never played a percussion instrument before, this is
the recommended way of playing. With mallets, it is very
easy to produce beautiful notes without any effort. Mallets
bounce easily on the notes, producing a very clear and deep
sound.

Playing with your hands is more enjoyable, but as mentioned, it requires more technical
skill and practice. Most popular models of tongue drum have 6 to 15 notes and come in
different sizes, from 5.5 to 20 inches. They can be in many tones: major, minor, pentaton-
ic. Some drums have hole octave notes, while some do not. Very often small drums do not
include the note F but the notes C, D and E exist in two different octaves. If your model
doesn't have the F note (4), just skip the songs that need this note. Fortunately, most songs
assembled here don't use it.

It is important to consider the size of your steel tongue drum. Generally, a smaller drum
produces a different sound than that of the larger ones. Most people prefer the sounds
produced by larger tongue drums. If you're looking for a more powerful and intense
sound, the bigger the instrument, the more volume and reverb it will produce.

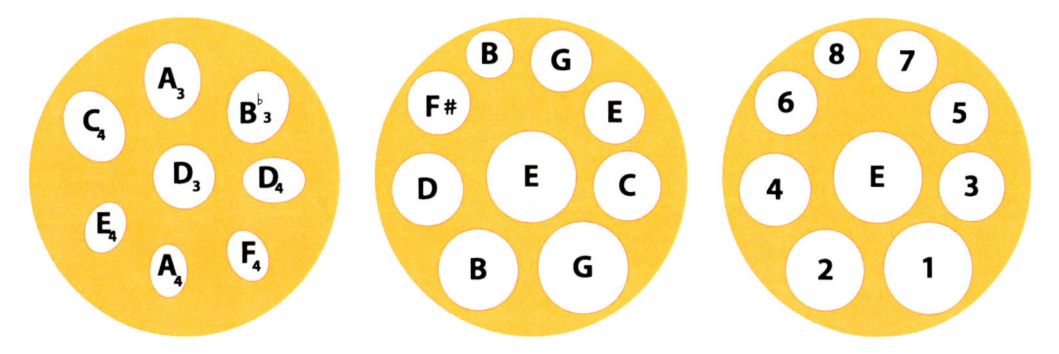

Our book is for those who want to try playing simple popular tunes, and not just relax.
As mentioned, the keys are tuned in different notes and you need to understand what notes
your particular instrument has. Depending on your instrument, you can skip those songs
that contain notes that are missing on your specific drum.

To understand what notes your drum has, you need to look at the instructions. Sometimes
the notes are indicated by numbers directly on the keys. Stickers with numbers are
sometimes included with the drum.

Hand Playing Technique

- Begin to play with mallets, and then play with your hands. Don't wear rings or any other jewelry while playing.
- Your finger should maintain contact with the surface of the drum for a very short time. The shorter the time of contact with the surface, the longer the sound becomes.
- The quicker your fingers bounce up the drum keys, the richer the overtones will be. Avoid putting your fingers in the middle of the tongue.
- Use the palm to produce force or to extinguish the sound.
- Experiment with different sounds and melodies. No rules - just play whatever you like.

Play by Number

For tongue drums that have numbered musical notation, numbers 1 to 7 represent the keys of the diatonic major scale. For example, a C Major scale would be:

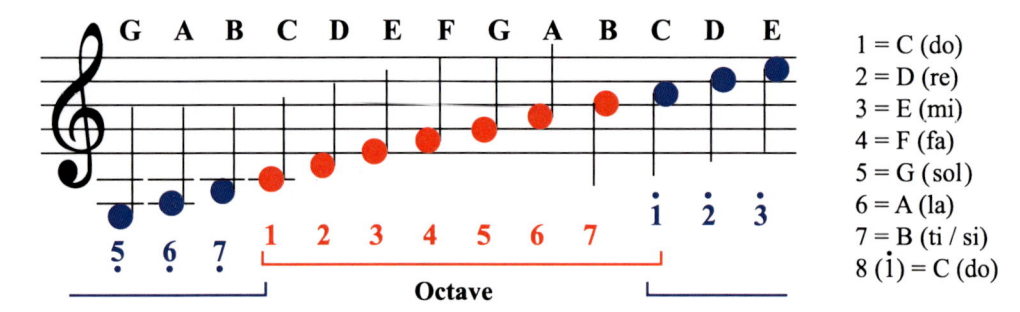

1 = C (do)
2 = D (re)
3 = E (mi)
4 = F (fa)
5 = G (sol)
6 = A (la)
7 = B (ti / si)
8 (1̇) = C (do)

Dots above or below the numbers indicate a note from a higher or lower octave, respectively.

Your drum can be numbered from 1 to 8, where 8 is note C of the next octave. We use number 1 with a dot above the digit for this note because the most popular models of tongue drums use this numeration.

This book is aimed at those who want to add popular melodies to their experimentation. All songs in this book have been written without using the classic music score system, because it is for the absolute beginner who cannot read sheet music.

We use circles with numbers because most modern tongue drums have numbers engraved or painted on their keys.
We do not show the note duration - we just group the circles closer to each other to show the rhythms. You can experiment with duration on your own.

Because most tongue drums include and are tuned to involve the notes of the main octave, all songs from this book are possible to play in one octave. If you have less than 1 octave of keys on your drum, you may need to skip some songs. Each tongue drum is very different and it is impossible to accommodate songs for all kinds of tongue drums in one book.
This book includes very simple, popular children's and folk songs, but even well-known children's songs played on the drum will create an unusual magical sound.

Rub-a-Dub-Dub

① ① ① ① ① ③ ③ ③ ③

Rub-a-dub-dub, three men in a tub,

③ ⑤ ⑤ ⑤ ⑤ ⑤ ⑤ ⑤

And who do you think they be?

⑤ i̇ i̇ i̇ ⑤ ⑤ ⑤

The butcher, the baker, the

③ ③ ③ ① ① ①

candlestick maker, and

⑤ ⑤ ④ ③ ② ①

all of them gone to sea.

*The dots above the numbers mean the notes of another octave (not the main octave).

The Wheels on the Bus

① ④ ④ ④ ④ ⑥ i̇ ⑥ ④

The wheels on the bus go round and round.

⑤ ③ ① i̇ ⑥ ④

Round and round. Round and round.

① ④ ④ ④ ④ ⑥ i̇ ⑥ ④

The wheels on the bus go round and round.

⑤ ① ① ④

Round and round.

Miss Mary Mack

(5) (6) (7) (1) (1) (1)
Miss Mary Mack, Mack, Mack,

(5) (6) (7) (1) (1) (1)
all dressed in black, black, black,

(5) (6) (7) (1) (1) (1) (1) (1) (1)
with silver buttons, buttons, buttons

(5) (6) (7) (1) (1) (1)
all down her back, back, back!

Happy Birthday

①①②　①④③

Happy birthday to you,

①①②　①⑤④

Happy birthday to you,

①①i　⑥④④③②

Happy birthday dear Mary,

i i ⑥　④⑤④

Happy birthday to you!

9

Doggie Doggie

⑤ ⑤ ③ ③ ⑤ ⑤ ③

Doggie, doggie, where's your bone?

⑤ ⑤ ⑤ ③ ⑥ ⑤ ⑤ ③

Somebody stole it from your home.

⑤ ③ ⑥ ⑤ ③

Who has my bone?

⑤ ③ ⑥ ⑤ ③

I have your bone.

Mary Had a Little Lamb

③ ② ① ② ③ ③ ③
Mary had a little lamb,
② ② ② ③ ⑤ ⑤
Little lamb, little lamb,
③ ② ① ② ③ ③ ③
Mary had a little lamb,
③ ② ② ③ ② ①
Its fleece was white as snow.

Oh We Can Play on the Big Bass Drum

①　③　⑤　⑤　⑤　⑤　⑥　⑤　③　①
Oh　　we　can　play on the　big bass drum,

①　i̇　i̇　i̇　⑦　⑥　⑥　⑤
And this　is the　　music　to　it.

③　　③　　②　①②③③②
Boom, boom, boom goes the big bass drum,

⑤　i̇　　①　②　③　②　①
And that's　the　way　we　do　it.

12

Twinkle, Twinkle Little Star

① ① ⑤ ⑤ ⑥ ⑥ ⑤

Twin-kle, twin-kle lit-tle star,

④ ④ ③ ③ ② ② ①

How I won-der what you are.

⑤ ⑤ ④ ④ ③ ③ ②

Up a-bove the world so high,

⑤ ⑤ ④ ④ ③ ③ ②

Like a dia-mond in the sky.

A Hunting We Will Go

⑦ ⑥ ⑤ ⑤ ⑤ ⑤
A hunting we will go,

⑤ ⑤ ⑥ ⑥ ⑥ ⑥
A hunting we will go.

⑥ ⑥ ⑦ ⑦ ⑦ ⑦
We'll catch a fox and put

① ① ① ① ① ①
him in a box. And then

⑦ ⑦ ⑥ ⑥ ⑤
we'll let him go.

14

Kookaburra

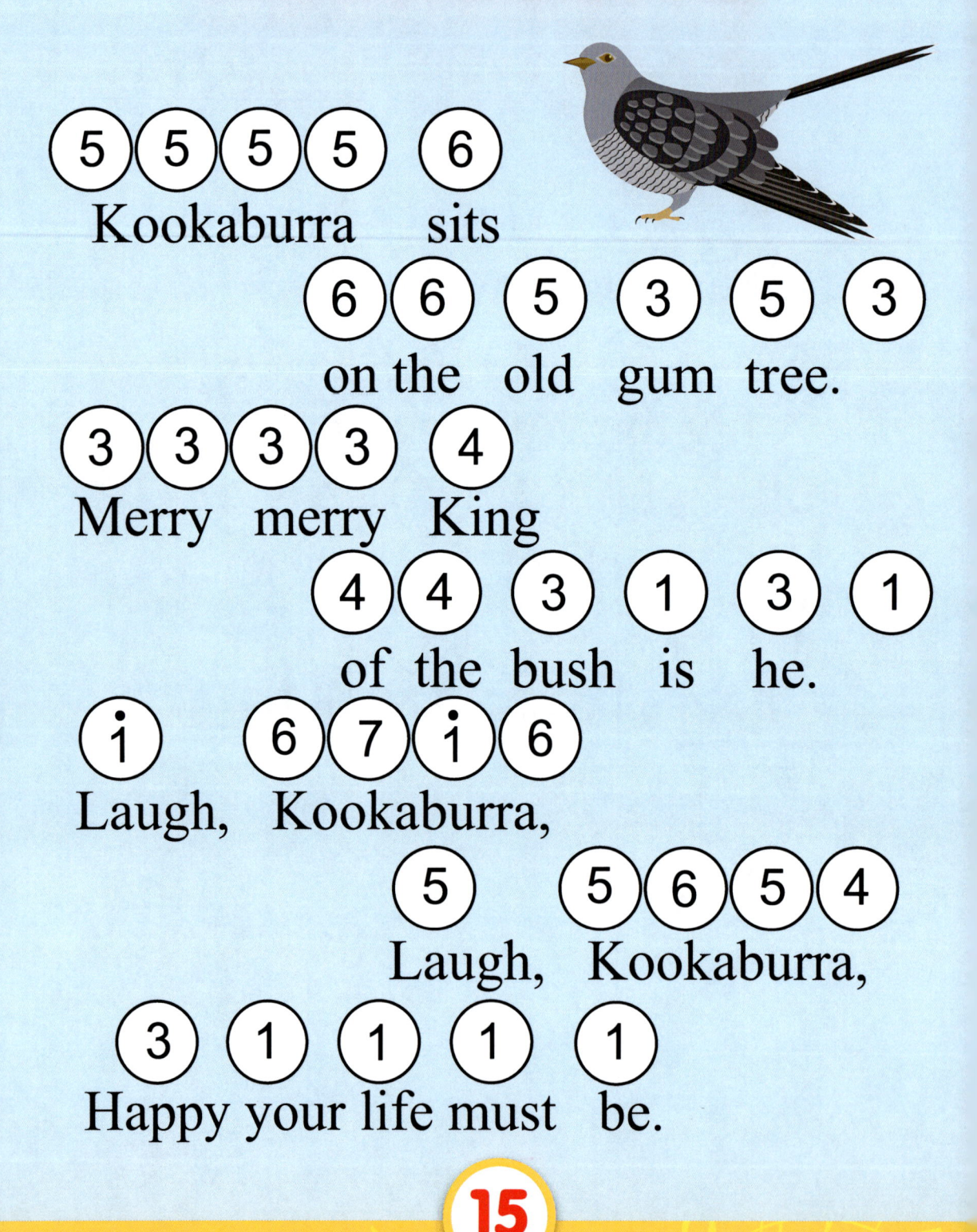

⑤ ⑤ ⑤ ⑤ ⑥
Kookaburra sits

⑥ ⑥ ⑤ ③ ⑤ ③
on the old gum tree.

③ ③ ③ ③ ④
Merry merry King

④ ④ ③ ① ③ ①
of the bush is he.

①̇ ⑥ ⑦ ①̇ ⑥
Laugh, Kookaburra,

⑤ ⑤ ⑥ ⑤ ④
Laugh, Kookaburra,

③ ① ① ① ①
Happy your life must be.

15

Ode to Joy

③ ③ ④ ⑤ ⑤ ④ ③ ②
① ① ② ③ ③ ② ②
③ ③ ④ ⑤ ⑤ ④ ③ ②
① ① ② ③ ② ① ①
② ② ③ ① ② ③ ④ ③ ①
② ③ ④ ③ ② ① ② ⑤
③ ③ ④ ⑤ ⑤ ④ ③ ②
① ① ② ③ ② ① ①

16

Do You Know the Muffin Man?

① ① ④ ④ ⑤ ⑥ ④ ④

Oh, do you know the muf-fin man,

③ ② ⑤ ⑤ ④ ③ ① ①

The muf-fin man, the muf-fin man.

① ① ④ ④ ⑤ ⑥ ④ ④

Oh, do you know the muf-fin man.

④ ⑤ ⑤ ① ① ④

That lives on Dru-ry Lane?

Old Bald Eagle

④ ④ ④ ④ ④ ④ ①

Old bald eagle sail around,

④ ③ ④ ⑤

daylight is gone.

③ ③ ③ ③ ③ ③ ①

Old bald eagle sail around,

⑥ ⑥ ⑤ ④

daylight is gone.

Two bald eagles…

Three bald eagles…

Four bald eagles…

18

La Cucaracha

1	1	1	4		6		
1	1	1	4		6		

4		4	3	3	2	2	1

1	1	1	3		5		
1	1	1	3		5		
i		i	i	i	6	5	4

19

A Sailor Went to Sea

(5) (i) (5) (6) (5) (3) (5) (5) (5)
A sailor went to sea, sea, sea, to

(6) (5) (6) (7) (i) (i) (i) (5)
see what he could see, see, see, but

(i) (5) (6) (5) (3) (5) (5) (5) (5)
all that he could see, see, see, was the

(6) (6) (6) (6) (7) (7) (i) (i) (i)
bottom of the deep blue sea, sea, sea.

20

Are You Sleeping?

① ② ③ ①　① ② ③ ①
Are you sleeping, are you sleeping?

③ ④ ⑤　③ ④ ⑤
Brother John, Brother John?

⑤ ⑥ ⑤ ④ ③ ①
Morning bells are ringing,

⑤ ⑥ ⑤ ④ ③ ①
Morning bells are ringing

② ⑤ ①　② ⑤ ①
Ding ding dong, ding ding dong.

Another Version

⑤ ⑥ ⑦ ⑤ ⑤ ⑥ ⑦ ⑤
Are you sleeping, are you sleeping?
⑦ ①̇ ②̇ ⑦ ①̇ ②̇
Brother John, Brother John?
②̇ ③̇ ②̇ ①̇ ⑦ ⑤
Morning bells are ringing,
②̇ ③̇ ②̇ ①̇ ⑦ ⑤
Morning bells are ringing
⑥ ② ⑤ ⑥ ② ⑤
Ding ding dong, ding ding dong.

The Mulberry Bush

④ ④ ④ ④ ⑥ İ İ ⑥ ④
Here we go round the mulberry bush,

④ ⑤ ⑤ ⑤ ⑤ ⑥ ⑤ ⑤ ③ ①
the mulberry bush, the mulberry bush,

④ ④ ④ ④ ⑥ İ İ ⑥ ④
Here we go round the mulberry bush,

④ ⑤ ⑤ ① ② ③ ④ ④
so early in the morning.

23

Old MacDonald Had a Farm

⑤ ⑤ ⑤ ② ③ ③ ②
Old McDonald had a farm.
⑦ ⑦ ⑥ ⑥ ⑤
E - I - E - I - O

② ⑤ ⑤ ⑤ ② ③ ③ ②
And on that farm he had a cow.
⑦ ⑦ ⑥ ⑥ ⑤
E - I - E - I - O

② ② ⑤ ⑤ ⑤
With a moo moo here.
② ② ⑤ ⑤ ⑤
With a moo moo there.
⑤ ⑤ ⑤
Here a moo.
⑤ ⑤ ⑤
There a moo.
⑤ ⑤ ⑤ ⑤ ⑤ ⑤
Everywhere a moo moo.
⑤ ⑤ ⑤ ② ③ ③ ②
Old McDonald had a farm.
⑦ ⑦ ⑥ ⑥ ⑤
E - I - E - I - O

Bim Bum Biddy

①　⑤　①　⑤　⑥　⑤　④　⑥　⑤　③　④
Bim bum, bim bum, biddy　biddy　bum, biddy

⑤　④　③　④　③　②　③　⑤
bum,　biddy　biddy bum　bim bum.

①　⑤　①　⑤　⑥　⑤　④　⑥　⑤　③　④
Bim bum, bim bum, biddy　biddy　bum, biddy

⑤　④　③　④　③　②　③　①
bum,　biddy　biddy bum　bim bum.

i̇　⑤　⑥　⑤　④　⑥　⑤　③　④
Bim　bum,　biddy　biddy　bum, biddy

⑤　④　③　④　③　②　③　⑤
bum,　biddy　biddy bum　bim bum.

i̇　⑤　⑥　⑤　④　⑥　⑤　③　④
Bim　bum,　biddy　biddy　bum, biddy

⑤　④　③　④　③　②　③　①
bum,　biddy　biddy bum　bim bum.

25

London Bridge Is Falling Down

⑤ ⑥ ⑤ ④ ③ ④ ⑤

London Bridge is falling down,

② ③ ④ ③ ④ ⑤

Falling down, falling down.

⑤ ⑥ ⑤ ④ ③ ④ ⑤

London Bridge is falling down,

② ⑤ ③ ①

My fair lady.

Jingle Bells

③ ③ ③   ③ ③ ③
Jingle bells, jingle bells,
③ ⑤ ① ② ③
Jingle all the way.
④ ④ ④ ④ ④ ③ ③
Oh, what fun it is to ride
③ ③ ② ② ③ ② ⑤
In a one horse open sleigh.
③ ③ ③   ③ ③ ③
Jingle bells, jingle bells,
③ ⑤ ① ② ③
Jingle all the way.
④ ④ ④ ④ ④ ③ ③
Oh, what fun it is to ride
③ ⑤ ⑤ ④ ② ①
In a one horse open sleigh.

Tinga Layo

③ ⑤ ⑥ ⑤ ④ ④ ④ ⑤ ④ ③
Tinga Layo, come, little donkey, come,

③ ⑤ ⑥ ⑤ ② ② ② ③ ② ①
Tinga Layo, come, little donkey, come,

⑤ i̇ ⑦ ⑥ ④ ⑦ ⑥ ⑤
My donkey walk, my donkey talk,

③ ⑥ ⑤ ④ ③ ② ⑤ ④ ③
My donkey cut with a knife and fork.

③ ⑤ ⑥ ⑤ ④ ④ ④ ⑤ ④ ③
Tinga Layo, come, little donkey, come,

③ ⑤ ⑥ ⑤ ② ② ② ③ ② ①
Tinga Layo, come, little donkey, come,

⑤ i̇ ⑦ ② ② ② ③ ② ①
My donkey, come, little donkey, come.

28

Itsy Bitsy Spider

①①①①②③③
The itsy-bitsy spider
③　②①②③　①
Climbed up the water spout.
③　③　④　⑤
Down came the rain
⑤　④　③④⑤　③
And washed the spider out.
①①②③
Out came the sun
③②①②③①
And dried up all the rain
①①①①②③③
And the itsy-bitsy spider
③　②①　②　③①
Climbed up the spout again.

29

We Wish You a Merry Christmas

① ④ ④ ⑤ ④ ③ ② ②

We wish you a Mer-ry Christ-mas,

② ⑤ ⑤ ⑥ ⑤ ④ ③ ①

We wish you a Mer-ry Christ-mas,

① ⑥ ⑥ ⑥ ⑥ ⑤ ④ ②

We wish you a Mer-ry Christ-mas,

① ① ② ⑤ ③ ④

And a Hap-py New Year!

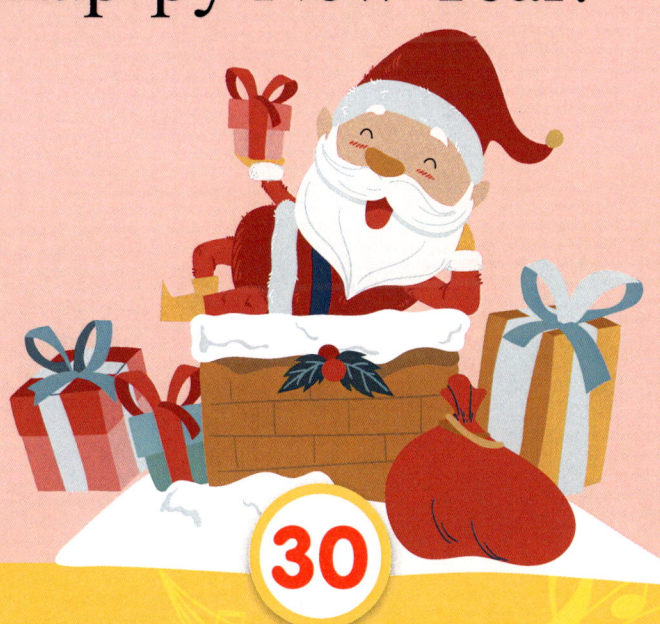

Brahms' Lullaby

③ ③⑤ ③ ③ ⑤
Lullaby, and good night,
③ ⑤ ① ⑦ ⑥ ⑥ ⑤
With pink roses bedight,
② ③④ ② ② ③ ④
With lilies o'er spread,
② ④ ⑦ ⑥ ⑤ ⑦ ①
Is my baby's sweet head.
① ① ① ⑥ ④ ⑤
Lay you down now, and rest,
③ ① ④ ⑤ ⑥ ⑤
May your slumber be blessed!
① ① ① ⑥ ④ ⑤
Lay you down now, and rest,
③ ① ④ ③ ② ①
May your slumber be blessed!

Ninety-Nine Bottles

④ ④ ④ ① ① ① ④ ④ ④ ④
Ninety-nine bottles of pop on the wall,

⑤ ⑤ ⑤ ② ② ② ⑤
Ninety-nine bottles of pop.

③ ③ ③ ③ ③ ③ ③
Take one down, pass it around,

① ① ① ② ② ③ ④ ④ ④ ④
Ninety-eight bottles of pop on the wall.

No more bottles of pop on the wall,
no more bottles of pop.
Go to the store and buy some more,
99 bottles of pop on the wall…

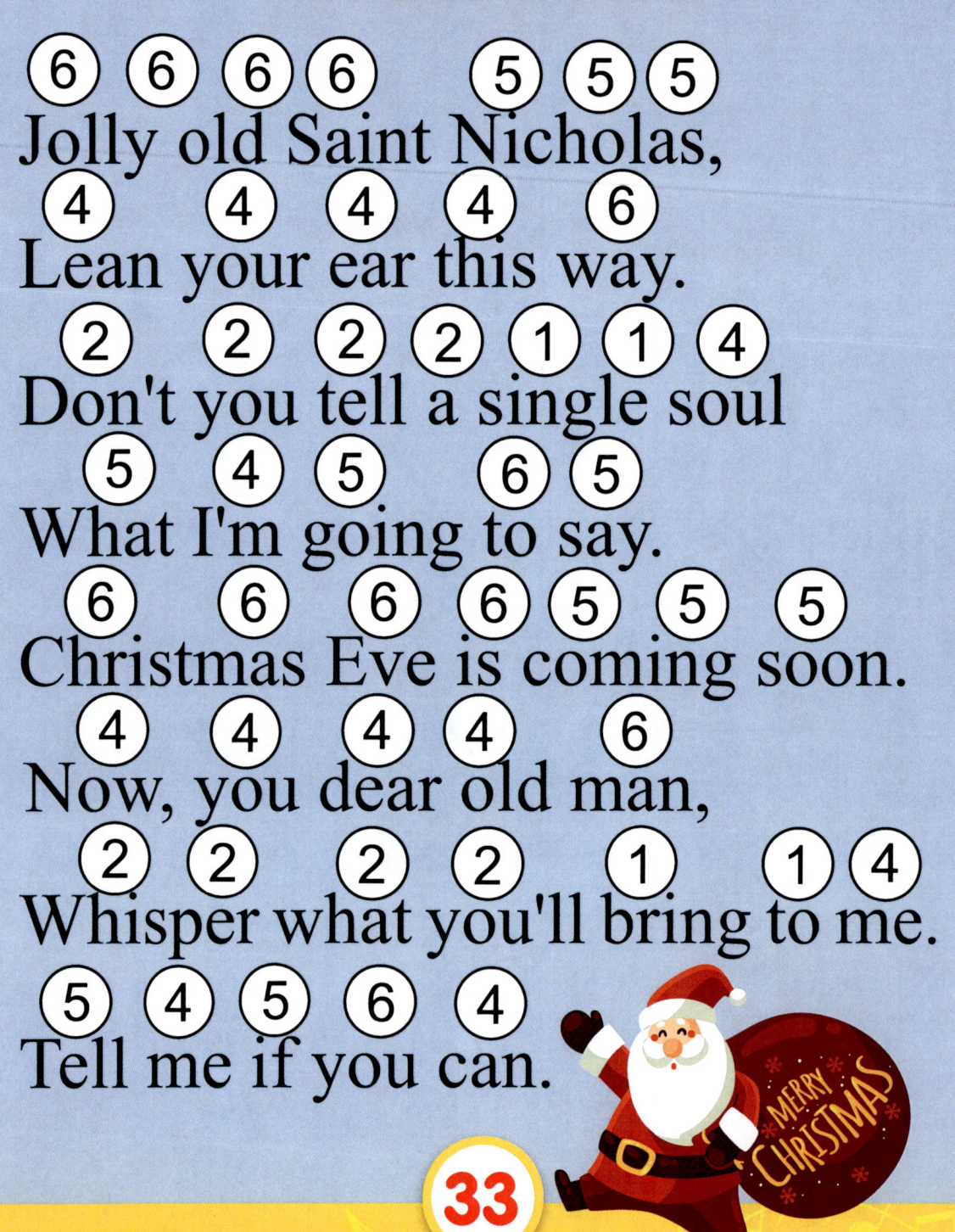

Jolly Old Saint Nicholas

⑥ ⑥ ⑥ ⑥   ⑤ ⑤ ⑤
Jolly old Saint Nicholas,
④   ④   ④   ④   ⑥
Lean your ear this way.
② ② ② ② ① ① ④
Don't you tell a single soul
⑤   ④ ⑤   ⑥ ⑤
What I'm going to say.
⑥   ⑥   ⑥ ⑥ ⑤ ⑤ ⑤
Christmas Eve is coming soon.
④   ④   ④   ④   ⑥
Now, you dear old man,
② ② ② ② ① ① ④
Whisper what you'll bring to me.
⑤ ④ ⑤ ⑥ ④
Tell me if you can.

33

Oh! Susannah

① ② ③ ⑤ ⑤ ⑥ ⑤ ③
Well! I come from A-la-ba-ma

① ② ③ ③ ② ① ②
With my ban-jo on my knee,

① ② ③ ⑤ ⑤ ⑥ ⑤ ③
I'm going to Louis-i-a-na

① ② ③ ③ ② ② ①
My true love for to see.

④ ④ ⑥ ⑥
Oh! Su-san-nah,

⑤   ⑤ ③ ① ②
Don't you cry for me

① ② ③ ⑤ ⑤ ⑥ ⑤ ③
I come from A-la-ba-ma

① ② ③ ③ ② ② ①
With my Ban-jo on my knee.

34

Row, Row, Row Your Boat

①　①　①　②　③
Row, row, row your boat,
③　②　③　④　⑤
Gently down the stream.
①̇ ①̇ ①̇ ⑤ ⑤ ⑤ ③ ③ ③ ① ① ①
Merrily, merrily, merrily, merrily,
⑤　④　③　②　①
Life is but a dream.

Acka Backa

(5) (5) (6) (6)   (5) (5) (3) (3)
Acka Backa   soda cracker

(5) (5) (6) (6)   (5)
Acka Backa   Boo.

(5) (5) (6) (6)   (5) (5) (3) (3)
Acka Backa   soda cracker

(5) (5) (3)
Out goes you!

Hot Cross Buns

③ ② ①

Hot Cross Buns,

③ ② ①

Hot Cross Buns,

① ① ① ①

One a pen - ny,

② ② ② ②

Two a pen - ny,

③ ② ①

Hot Cross Buns.

Bell Horses

⑤ ③ ③   ⑤ ③ ③
Bell horses, bell horses,

⑤ ⑤ ⑥ ⑥ ⑤
What's the time of day?

⑤ ⑤ ③ ⑤ ⑤ ③
One o'clock, two o'clock,

⑤ ⑤ ⑥ ⑥ ⑤
Time to go away.

Made in United States
North Haven, CT
16 December 2022